Bliss Carman

By the Aurelian wall and other elegies

Bliss Carman

By the Aurelian wall and other elegies

ISBN/EAN: 9783337017644

Printed in Europe, USA, Canada, Australia, Japan

Cover: Foto ©Thomas Meinert / pixelio.de

More available books at **www.hansebooks.com**

By the Aurelian Wall

And Other Elegies

By Bliss Carman
Author of
Low Tide on Grand Pré, Behind the Arras,
Ballads of Lost Haven, &c.

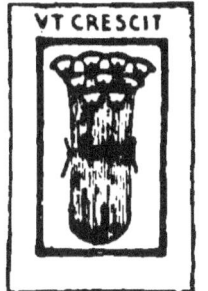

Lamson, Wolffe and Company
Boston, New York and London
MDCCCXCVIII

Copyright, 1898,
By Lamson, Wolffe and Company.

All rights reserved.

Norwood Press
J. S. Cushing & Co. — Berwick & Smith
Norwood Mass. U.S.A.

CONTENTS

By the Aurelian Wall, 9
The White Gull, 15
The Country of Har, 32
To Richard Lovelace, 42
A Seamark, 44
The Word of the Water, 57
Phillips Brooks, 59
John Eliot Bowen, 64
Henry George, 67
Ilicet, 70
To Raphael, 76
To P. V., 82
A Norse Child's Requiem, 87
In the Heart of the Hills, 91
An Afterword, 96
Seven Wind Songs, 102
Andrew Straton, 112
The Grave-Tree, 127

BY THE AURELIAN WALL

In Memory of John Keats

By the Aurelian Wall,
Where the long shadows of the centuries fall
From Caius Cestius' tomb,
A weary mortal seeking rest found room
For quiet burial,

Leaving among his friends
A book of lyrics.
Such untold amends
A traveller might make
In a strange country, bidden to partake
Before he farther wends;

By the Aurelian Wall

Who shyly should bestow
The foreign reed-flute they had seen him blow
And finger cunningly,
On one of the dark children standing by,
Then lift his cloak and go.

The years pass. And the child
Thoughtful beyond his fellows, grave and mild,
Treasures the rough-made toy,
Until one day he blows it for clear joy,
And wakes the music wild.

His fondness makes it seem
A thing first fashioned in delirious dream,
Some god had cut and tried,
And filled with yearning passion, and cast aside
On some far woodland stream,—

By the Aurelian Wall

After long years to be
Found by the stranger and brought over sea,
A marvel and delight
To ease the noon and pierce the dark blue night,
For children such as he.

He learns the silver strain
Wherewith the ghostly houses of gray rain
And lonely valleys ring,
When the untroubled whitethroats make the spring
A world without a stain;

Then on his river reed,
With strange and unsuspected notes that plead
Of their own wild accord
For utterances no bird's throat could afford,
Lifts it to human need.

By the Aurelian Wall

His comrades leave their play,
When calling and compelling far away
By river-slope and hill,
He pipes their wayward footsteps where he will,
All the long lovely day.

Even his elders come.
"Surely the child is elvish," murmur some,
And shake the knowing head;
"Give us the good old simple things instead,
Our fathers used to hum."

Others at the open door
Smile when they hear what they have hearkened for
These many summers now,
Believing they should live to learn somehow
Things never known before.

By the Aurelian Wall

But he can only tell
How the flute's whisper lures him with a spell,
Yet always just eludes
The lost perfection over which he broods;
And how he loves it well.

Till all the country-side,
Familiar with his piping far and wide,
Has taken for its own
That weird enchantment down the evening blown, —
Its glory and its pride.

And so his splendid name,
Who left the book of lyrics and small fame
Among his fellows then,
Spreads through the world like autumn — who knows when? —
Till all the hillsides flame.

By the Aurelian Wall

Grand Pré and Margaree
Hear it upbruited from the unresting sea;
And the small Gaspareau,
Whose yellow leaves repeat it, seems to know
A new felicity.

Even the shadows tall,
Walking at sundown through the plain, recall
A mound the grasses keep,
Where once a mortal came and found long sleep
By the Aurelian Wall.

THE WHITE GULL

For the Centenary of the Birth of Shelley

I

Up by the idling reef-set bell
The tide comes in;
And to the idle heart to-day
The wind has many things to say;
The sea has many a tale to tell
His younger kin.

By the Aurelian Wall

For we are his, bone of his bone,
Breath of his breath;
The doom tides sway us at their will;
The sky of being rounds us still;
And over us at last is blown
The wind of death.

II

A hundred years ago to-day
There came a soul,
A pilgrim of the perilous light,
Treading the spheral paths of night,
On whom the word and vision lay
With dread control.

The White Gull

Now the pale Summer lingers near,
And talks to me
Of all her wayward journeyings,
And the old, sweet, forgotten things
She loved and lost and dreamed of here
By the blue sea.

The great cloud-navies, one by one,
Bend sails and fill
From ports below the round sea-verge;
I watch them gather and emerge,
And steer for havens of the sun
Beyond the hill.

By the Aurelian Wall

The gray sea-horses troop and roam;
The shadows fly
Along the wind-floor at their heels;
And where the golden daylight wheels,
A white gull searches the blue dome
With keening cry.

And something, Shelley, like thy fame
Dares the wide morn
In that sea-rover's glimmering flight,
As if the Northland and the night
Should hear thy splendid valiant name
Put scorn to scorn.

The White Gull

III

Thou heart of all the hearts of men,
Tameless and free,
And vague as that marsh-wandering fire,
Leading the world's outworn desire
A night march down this ghostly fen
From sea to sea!

Through this divided camp of dream
Thy feet have passed,
As one who should set hand to rouse
His comrades from their heavy drowse;
For only their own deeds redeem
God's sons at last.

By the Aurelian Wall

But the dim world will dream and sleep
Beneath thy hand,
As poppies in the windy morn,
Or valleys where the standing corn
Whispers when One goes forth to reap
The weary land.

O captain of the rebel host,
Lead forth and far!
Thy toiling troopers of the night
Press on the unavailing fight;
The sombre field is not yet lost,
With thee for star.

The White Gull

Thy lips have set the hail and haste
Of clarions free
To bugle down the wintry verge
Of time forever, where the surge
Thunders and crumbles on a waste
And open sea.

IV

Did the cold Norns who pattern life
With haste and rest
Take thought to cheer their pilgrims on
Through trackless twilights vast and wan,
Across the failure and the strife,
From quest to quest, —

By the Aurelian Wall

Set their last kiss upon thy face,
And let thee go
To tell the haunted whisperings
Of unimaginable things,
Which plague thy fellows with a trace
They cannot know?

So they might fashion and send forth
Their house of doom,
Through the pale splendor of the night,
In vibrant, hurled, impetuous flight,
A resonant meteor of the North
From gloom to gloom.

The White Gull

V

I think thou must have wandered far
With Spring for guide,
And heard the shy-born forest flowers
Talk to the wind among the showers,
Through sudden doorways left ajar
When the wind sighed;

Thou must have heard the marching sweep
Of blown white rain
Go volleying up the icy kills, —
And watched with Summer when the hills
Muttered of freedom in their sleep
And slept again.

By the Aurelian Wall

Surely thou wert a lonely one,
Gentle and wild;
And the round sun delayed for thee
In the red moorlands by the sea,
When Tyrian Autumn lured thee on,
A wistful child,

To rove the tranquil, vacant year,
From dale to dale;
And the great Mother took thy face
Between her hands for one long gaze,
And bade thee follow without fear
The endless trail.

The White Gull

And thy clear spirit, half forlorn,
Seeking its own,
Dwelt with the nomad tents of rain,
Marched with the gold-red ranks of grain,
Or ranged the frontiers of the morn,
And was alone.

VI

One brief perturbed and glorious day!
How couldst thou learn
The quiet of the forest sun,
Where the dark, whispering rivers run
The journey that hath no delay
And no return?

By the Aurelian Wall

And yet within thee flamed and sang
The dauntless heart,
Knowing all passion and the pain
On man's imperious disdain,
Since God's great part in thee gave pang
To earth's frail part.

It held the voices of the hills
Deep in its core;
The wandering shadows of the sea
Called to it, — would not let it be;
The harvest of those barren rills
Was in its store.

The White Gull

Thine was a love that strives and calls
Outcast from home,
Burning to free the soul of man
With some new life. How strange, a ban
Should set thy sleep beneath the walls
Of changeless Rome!

VII

More soft, I deem, from spring to spring,
Thy sleep would be
Where this far western headland lies
With its imperial azure skies,
Under thee hearing beat and swing
The eternal sea.

By the Aurelian Wall

Where all the livelong brooding day
And all night long,
The far sea-journeying wind should come
Down to the doorway of thy home,
To lure thee ever the old way
With the old song.

But the dim forest would so house
Thy heart so dear,
Even the low surf of the rain,
Where ghostly centuries complain,
Might beat against thy door and rouse
No heartache here.

The White Gull

For here the thrushes, calm, supreme,
Forever reign,
Whose gloriously kingly golden throats
Regather their forgotten notes
In keys where lurk no ruin of dream,
No tinge of pain.

And here the ruthless noisy sea,
With the tide's will,
The strong gray wrestler, should in vain
Put forth his hand on thee again —
Lift up his voice and call to thee,
And thou be still.

By the Aurelian Wall

For thou hast overcome at last;
And fate and fear
And strife and rumor now no more
Vex thee by any wind-vexed shore,
Down the strewn ways thy feet have passed
Far, far from here.

VIII

Up by the idling, idling bell
The tide comes in;
And to the restless heart to-day
The wind has many things to say;
The sea has many a tale to tell
His younger kin.

The White Gull

The gray sea-horses troop and roam;
The shadows fly
Along the wind-floor at their heels;
And where the golden daylight wheels,
A white gull searches the blue dome
With keening cry.

THE COUNTRY OF HAR

For the Centenary of Blake's "Songs of Innocence"

Once a hundred years ago
There was a light in London town,
For an angel of the snow
Walked her street sides up and down.

As a visionary boy
He put forth his hand to smite
Songs of innocence and joy
From the crying chords of night,

The Country of Har

Like a muttering of thunder
Heard beneath the polar star;
For his soul was all a-wonder
At the calling vales of Har.

He, a traveller by day
And a pilgrim of the sun,
Took his uncompanioned way
Where the journey is not done.

Where no mortal might aspire
His clear heart was set to climb,
To the uplands of desire
And the river wells of time.

By the Aurelian Wall

Home he wandered to the valley
Where the springs of morning are,
And the sea-bright cohorts rally
On the twilit plains of Har.

There he found the Book of Thel
In the lily-garth of bliss,
Fashioned, how no man can tell,
As a white windflower is:

Like the lulling of a sigh
Uttered in the trembling grass,
When a shower is gone by,
And the sweeping shadows pass, —

The Country of Har

Through the hyacinthine weather,
Wheel them down without a jar, —
Heaving all the dappled heather
In the streaming vales of Har.

There was manna in the rain;
And above the rills, a voice:
"Son of mine, dost thou complain?
I will make thee to rejoice.

"Thou shalt be a child to men,
With confusion on thy speech;
And the worlds within thy ken
Shall not lie within thy reach.

By the Aurelian Wall

"But the rainbirds shall discover,
And the daffodils unbar,
Quiet waters for their lover
On the shining plains of Har.

"April rain and iron frost
Shall make flowers to thy hand;
Every field thy feet have crossed
Shall revive from death's command.

"Hunting with a leash of wind
Through the corners of the earth,
Take the hounds of Spring to find
The forgotten trails of mirth;

The Country of Har

"For the lone child-heart is dying
Of a love no time can mar,
Hearing not a voice replying
From the gladder vales of Har.

"Flame thy heart forth! Yet, no haste:
Have not I prepared for thee
The king's chambers of the East
And the wind halls of the sea?

"Be a gospeller of things
Nowhere written through the wild,
With that gloaming call of Spring's,
When old secrets haunt the child.

By the Aurelian Wall

"Let the bugler of my going
Wake no clarion of war;
For the paper reeds are blowing
On the river plains of Har."

Centuries of soiled renown
To the roaring dark have gone:
There is woe in London town,
And a crying for the dawn.

April frost and iron rain
Ripen the dead fruit of lust,
And the sons of God remain
The dream children of the dust,

The Country of Har

For their heart hath in derision,
And their jeers have mocked afar,
The delirium of vision
From the holy vales of Har.

Once in Autumn came a dream;
The white Herald of the North,
Faring West to ford my stream,
Passed my lodge and bade me forth;

Glad I rose and went with him,
With my shoulder in his hand;
The auroral world grew dim,
And the idle harvest land.

By the Aurelian Wall

Then I saw the warder lifting
From its berg the Northern bar,
And eternal snows were drifting
On the wind-bleak plains of Har.

"Listen humbly," said my guide.
"I am drear, for I am death,"
Whispered Snow; but Wind replied,
"I outlive thee by a breath,

I am Time." And then I heard,
Dearer than all wells of dew,
One gray golden-shafted bird
Hail the uplands; so I knew

The Country of Har

Spring, the angel of our sorrow,
Tarrying so seeming far,
Should return with some long morrow
In the calling vales of Har.

TO RICHARD LOVELACE

Ah, Lovelace, what desires have sway
In the white shadow of your heart,
Which no more measures day by day,
Nor sets the years apart?

How many seasons for your sake
Have taught men over, age by age,
"Stone walls do not a prison make,
Nor iron bars a cage!"—

To Richard Lovelace

Since that first April when you fared
Into the Gatehouse, well content,
Caring for nothing so you cared
For honor and for Kent.

How many, since the April rain
Beat drear and blossomless and hoar
Through London, when you left Shoe Lane,
A-marching to no war!

Till now, with April on the sea,
And sunshine in the woven year,
The rain-winds loose from reverie
A lyric and a cheer.

A SEAMARK

A Threnody for Robert Louis Stevenson

Cold, the dull cold! What ails the sun,
And takes the heart out of the day?
What makes the morning look so mean,
The Common so forlorn and gray?

The wintry city's granite heart
Beats on in iron mockery,
And like the roaming mountain rains,
I hear the thresh of feet go by.

A Seamark

It is the lonely human surf
Surging through alleys chill with grime,
The muttering churning ceaseless floe
Adrift out of the North of time.

Fades, it all fades! I only see
The poster with its reds and blues
Bidding the heart stand still to take
Its desolating stab of news.

That intimate and magic name:
"Dead in Samoa." . . . Cry your cries,
O city of the golden dome,
Under the gray Atlantic skies!

By the Aurelian Wall

But I have wander-biddings now.
Far down the latitudes of sun,
An island mountain of the sea,
Piercing the green and rosy zone,

Goes up into the wondrous day.
And there the brown-limbed island men
Are bearing up for burial,
Within the sun's departing ken,

The master of the roving kind.
And there where time will set no mark
For his irrevocable rest,
Under the spacious melting dark,

A Seamark

With all the nomad tented stars
About him, they have laid him down
Above the crumbling of the sea,
Beyond the turmoil of renown.

O all you hearts about the world
In whom the truant gipsy blood,
Under the frost of this pale time,
Sleeps like the daring sap and flood

That dream of April and reprieve!
You whom the haunted vision drives,
Incredulous of home and ease,
Perfection's lovers all your lives!

By the Aurelian Wall

You whom the wander-spirit loves
To lead by some forgotten clue
Forever vanishing beyond
Horizon brinks forever new;

The road, unmarked, ordained, whereby
Your brothers of the field and air
Before you, faithful, blind and glad,
Emerged from chaos pair by pair;

The road whereby you too must come,
In the unvexed and fabled years
Into the country of your dream,
With all your knowledge in arrears!

A Seamark

You who can never quite forget
Your glimpse of Beauty as she passed,
The well-head where her knee was pressed,
The dew wherein her foot was cast;

O you who bid the paint and clay
Be glorious when you are dead,
And fit the plangent words in rhyme
Where the dark secret lurks unsaid;

You brethren of the light-heart guild,
The mystic fellowcraft of joy,
Who tarry for the news of truth,
And listen for some vast ahoy

By the Aurelian Wall

Blown in from sea, who crowd the wharves
With eager eyes that wait the ship
Whose foreign tongue may fill the world
With wondrous tales from lip to lip;

Our restless loved adventurer,
On secret orders come to him,
Has slipped his cable, cleared the reef,
And melted on the white sea-rim.

O granite hills, go down in blue!
And like green clouds in opal calms,
You anchored islands of the main,
Float up your loom of feathery palms!

A Seamark

For deep within your dales, where lies
A valiant earthling stark and dumb,
This savage undiscerning heart
Is with the silent chiefs who come

To mourn their kin and bear him gifts, —
Who kiss his hand, and take their place,
This last night he receives his friends,
The journey-wonder on his face.

He "was not born for age." Ah no,
For everlasting youth is his!
Part of the lyric of the earth
With spring and leaf and blade he is.

By the Aurelian Wall

'Twill nevermore be April now
But there will lurk a thought of him
At the street corners, gay with flowers
From rainy valleys purple-dim.

O chiefs, you do not mourn alone!
In that stern North where mystery broods,
Our mother grief has many sons
Bred in those iron solitudes.

It does not help them, to have laid
Their coil of lightning under seas;
They are as impotent as you
To mend the loosened wrists and knees.

A Seamark

And yet how many a harvest night,
When the great luminous meteors flare
Along the trenches of the dusk,
The men who dwell beneath the Bear,

Seeing those vagrants of the sky
Float through the deep beyond their hark,
Like Arabs through the wastes of air, —
A flash, a dream, from dark to dark, —

Must feel the solemn large surmise:
By a dim vast and perilous way
We sweep through undetermined time,
Illumining this quench of clay,

By the Aurelian Wall

A moment staunched, then forth again.
Ah, not alone you climb the steep
To set your loving burden down
Against the mighty knees of sleep.

With you we hold the sombre faith
Where creeds are sown like rain at sea;
And leave the loveliest child of earth
To slumber where he longed to be.

His fathers lit the dangerous coast
To steer the daring merchant home;
His courage lights the dark'ning port
Where every sea-worn sail must come.

A Seamark

And since he was the type of all
That strain in us which still must fare,
The fleeting migrant of a day,
Heart-high, outbound for otherwhere,

Now therefore, where the passing ships
Hang on the edges of the noon,
And Northern liners trail their smoke
Across the rising yellow moon,

Bound for his home, with shuddering screw
That beats its strength out into speed,
Until the pacing watch descries
On the sea-line a scarlet seed

By the Aurelian Wall

Smolder and kindle and set fire
To the dark selvedge of the night,
The deep blue tapestry of stars,
Then sheet the dome in pearly light,

There in perpetual tides of day,
Where men may praise him and deplore,
The place of his lone grave shall be
A seamark set forevermore,

High on a peak adrift with mist,
And round whose bases, far beneath
The snow-white wheeling tropic birds,
The emerald dragon breaks his teeth.

THE WORD OF THE WATER

For the Unveiling of the Stevenson Fountain in San Francisco

God made me simple from the first,
And good to quench your body's thirst.
Think you he has no ministers
To glad that wayworn soul of yours?

Here by the thronging Golden Gate
For thousands and for you I wait,
Seeing adventurous sails unfurled
For the four corners of the world.

By the Aurelian Wall

Here passed one day, nor came again,
A prince among the tribes of men.
(For man, like me, is from his birth
A vagabond upon this earth.)

Be thankful, friend, as you pass on,
And pray for Louis Stevenson,
That by whatever trail he fare
He be refreshed in God's great care!

PHILLIPS BROOKS

THIS is the white winter day of his burial.
Time has set here of his toiling the span
Earthward, naught else. Cheer him out through
    the portal,
Heart-beat of Boston, our utmost in man!

Out in the broad open sun be his funeral,
Under the blue for the city to see.
Over the grieving crowd mourn for him, bugle!
Churches are narrow to hold such as he.

By the Aurelian Wall

Here on the steps of the temple he builded,
Rest him a space, while the great city square
Throngs with his people, his thousands, his
    mourners;
Tears for his peace and a multitude's prayer.

How comes it, think you, the town's traffic pauses
Thus at high noon? Can we wealthmongers grieve?
Here in the sad surprise greatest America
Shows for a moment her heart on her sleeve.

She who is said to give life-blood for silver,
Proves, without show, she sets higher than gold
Just the straight manhood, clean, gentle, and
    fearless,
Made in God's likeness once more as of old.

Phillips Brooks

Once more the crude makeshift law overproven, —
Soul pent from sin will seek God in despite;
Once more the gladder way wins revelation, —
Soul bent on God forgets evil outright.

Once more the seraph voice sounding to beauty,
Once more the trumpet tongue bidding, no fear!
Once more the new, purer plan's vindication, —
Man be God's forecast, and Heaven is here.

Bear him to burial, Harvard, thy hero!
Not on thy shoulders alone is he borne;
They of the burden go forth on the morrow,
Heavy and slow, through a world left forlorn.

By the Aurelian Wall

No grief for him, for ourselves the lamenting;
What giant arm to stay courage up now?
March we a thousand file up to the City,
Fellow with fellow linked, he taught us how!

Never dismayed at the dark nor the distance!
Never deployed for the steep nor the storm!
Hear him say, "Hold fast, the night wears to
    morning!
This God of promise is God to perform."

Up with thee, heart of fear, high as the heaven!
Thou hast known one wore this life without stain.
What if for thee and me, — street, Yard, or
    Common, —
Such a white captain appear not again!

Phillips Brooks

Fight on alone! Let the faltering spirit
Within thee recall how he carried a host,
Rearward and van, as Wind shoulders a dust-heap;
One Way till strife be done, strive each his most.

Take the last vesture of beauty upon thee,
Thou doubting world; and with not an eye dim
Say, when they ask if thou knowest a Saviour,
"Brooks was His brother, and we have known him."

JOHN ELIOT BOWEN

Here at the desk where once you sat,
Who wander now with poets dead
And summers gone, afield so far,
There sits a stranger in your stead.

Here day by day men come who knew
Your steadfast ways and loved you well;
And every comer with regret
Has some new thing of praise to tell.

John Eliot Bowen

The poet old, whose lyric heart
Is fresh as dew and bright as flame,
Longs for "his boy," and finds you not,
And goes the wistful way he came.

Here where you toiled without reproach,
Builded and loved and dreamed and planned,
At every door, on every page,
Lurks the tradition of your hand.

And if to you, like reverie,
There comes a thought of how they fare
Whose footsteps go the round you went
Of noisy street and narrow stair,

By the Aurelian Wall

Know they have learned a new desire,
Which puts unfaith and faltering by;
And triumph fills their dream because
One life was leal, one hope was high.

HENRY GEORGE

We are only common people,
And he was a man like us.
But he loved his fellows before himself;
And he died for me and you,
To redeem the world anew
From cruelty and greed —
For love the only creed,
For honor the only law.

By the Aurelian Wall

There once was a man of the people,
A man like you and me,
Who worked for his daily bread,
And he loved his fellows before himself.
But he died at the hands of the throng
To redeem the world from wrong,
And we call him the Son of God,
Because of the love he had.

And there was a man of the people,
Who sat in the people's chair,
And bade the slaves go free;
For he loved his fellows before himself.
They took his life; but his word
They could not take. It was heard
Over the beautiful earth,
A thunder and whisper of love.

Henry George

And there is no other way,
Since man of woman was born,
Than the way of the rebels and saints,
With loving and labor vast,
To redeem the world at last
From cruelty and greed;
For love is the only creed,
And honor the only law.

ILICET

Friends, let him rest
In midnight now.
Desire has gone
On the weary quest
With aching brow;
Until the dawn,
Friends, let him rest.

Ilicet

With a boy's desire
He set the cup
To his lips to drink;
The ruddy fire
Was lifted up
At day's cool brink,
With a boy's desire.

The heart of a boy!
He tasted life,
And the bitter sting
Of sorrow in joy,
Failure in strife,
Was pain to wring
The heart of a boy.

By the Aurelian Wall

In a childish whim,
He spilled the wine
Upon the floor, —
In beads on the brim
Was a glitter of brine, —
Then, out at the door
In a childish whim!

Out of the storm,
In the flickering light,
A broken glass
Lies on our warm
Hearthstone to-night,
While shadows pass
Out of the storm.

Ilicet

Friends, let him rest
In midnight now.
Desire has gone
On the weary quest
With aching brow:
Until the dawn,
Friends, let him rest.

In sorrow and shame
For the craven heart,
In manhood's breast
With valor's name,
Let him depart
Unto his rest
In sorrow and shame.

By the Aurelian Wall

In after years
God, who bestows
Or withholds the valor,
Shall wipe all tears —
Haply, who knows? —
From his face's pallor
In after years.

He could not learn
To fight with his peers
In sturdier fashion;
Let him return
Through the night with tears,
Stung with the passion
He could not learn.

Ilicet

All-bountiful, calm,
Where the great stars burn,
And the spring bloom smothers
The night with balm,
Let him return
To the silent Mother's
All-bountiful calm.

Friends, let him rest
In midnight now.
Desire has gone
On the weary quest
With aching brow:
Until the dawn,
Friends, let him rest.

TO RAPHAEL

Master of adored Madonnas,
What is this men say of thee?
Thou wert something less than honor's
Most exact epitome?

Yes, they say you loved too many,
Loved too often, loved too well.
Just as if there could be any
Over-loving, Raphael!

To Raphael

Was it, "Sir, and how came this tress,
Long and raven? Mine are gold!"
You should have made Art your mistress,
Lived an anchorite and old!

Ah, no doubt these dear good people
On familiar terms with God,
Could devise a parish steeple
Built to heaven without a hod.

You and Solomon and Cæsar
Were three fellows of a kind;
Not a woman but to please her
You would leave your soul behind.

By the Aurelian Wall

Those dead women with their beauty,
How they must have loved you well, —
Dared to make desire a duty,
With the heretics in hell!

And your brother, that Catullus,
What a plight he must be in,
If those silver songs that lull us
Were result of mortal sin!

If the artist were ungodly,
Prurient of mind and heart,
I must think they argue oddly
Who make shrines before his art.

To Raphael

Not the meanest aspiration
Ever sprung from soul depraved
Into art, but art's elation
Was the sanctity it craved.

Oh, no doubt you had your troubles,
Devils blue that blanched your hope.
I dare say your fancy's bubbles,
Breaking, had a taste of soap.

Did your lady-loves undo you
In some mediæval way?
Ah, my Raphael, here's to you!
It is much the same to-day.

By the Aurelian Wall

Did their tantalizing laughter
Make your wisdom overbold?
Were you fire at first; and after,
Did their kisses leave you cold?

Did some fine perfidious Nancy,
With the roses in her hair,
Play the marsh-fire to your fancy
Over quagmires of despair?

My poor boy, were there more flowers
In your Florence and your Rome,
Wasting through the gorgeous hours,
Than your two hands could bring home?

To Raphael

Be content ; you have your glory ;
Life was full and sleep is well.
What the end is of the story,
There's no paragraph to tell.

TO P. V.

So they would raise your monument,
Old vagabond of lovely earth?
Another answer without words
To Humdrum's, "What are poets worth?"

Not much we gave you when alive,
Whom now we lavishly deplore, —
A little bread, a little wine,
A little caporal — no more.

To P. V.

Here in our lodging of a day
You roistered till we were appalled;
Departing, in your room we found
A string of golden verses scrawled.

The princely manor-house of art,
A vagrant artist entertains;
And when he gets him to the road,
Behold, a princely gift remains.

Abashed, we set your name above
The purse-full patrons of our board;
Remind newcomers with a nudge,
"Verlaine took once what we afford!"

By the Aurelian Wall

The gardens of the Luxembourg,
Spreading beneath the brilliant sun,
Shall be your haunt of leisure now
When all your wander years are done.

There you shall stand, the very mien
You wore in Paris streets of old,
And ponder what a thing is life,
Or watch the chestnut blooms unfold.

There you will find, I dare surmise,
Another tolerance than ours,
The loving-kindness of the grass,
The tender patience of the flowers.

To P. V.

And every year, when May returns
To bring the golden age again,
And hope comes back with poetry
In your loved land across the Seine,

Some youth will come with foreign speech,
Bearing his dream from over sea,
A lover of your flawless craft,
Apprenticed to your poverty.

He will be mute before you there,
And mark those lineaments which tell
What stormy unrelenting fate
Had one who served his art so well.

By the Aurelian Wall

And there be yours, the livelong day,
Beyond the mordant reach of pain,
The little gospel of the leaves,
The *Nunc dimittis* of the rain!

A NORSE CHILD'S REQUIEM

SLEEP soundly, little Thorlak,
Where all thy peers have lain,
A hero of no battle,
A saint without a stain!

Thy courage be upon thee,
Unblemished by regret,
For that adventure whither
Thy tiny march was set.

By the Aurelian Wall

The sunshine be above thee,
With birds and winds and trees.
Thy way-fellows inherit
No better things than these.

And silence be about thee,
Turned back from this our war
To front alone the valley
Of night without a star.

The soul of love and valor,
Indifferent to fame,
Be with thee, heart of vikings,
Beyond the breath of blame.

A Norse Child's Requiem

Thy moiety of manhood
Unspent and fair, go down,
And, unabashed, encounter
Thy brothers of renown.

So modest in thy freehold
And tenure of the earth,
Thy needs, for all our meddling,
Are few and little worth.

Content thee, not with pity;
Be solaced, not with tears;
But when the whitethroats waken
Through the revolving years,

By the Aurelian Wall

Hereafter be that peerless
And dirging cadence, child,
Thy threnody unsullied,
Melodious, and wild.

Then winter be thy housing,
Thy lullaby the rain,
Thou hero of no battle,
Thou saint without a stain.

IN THE HEART OF THE HILLS

In the warm blue heart of the hills
My beautiful, beautiful one
Sleeps where he laid him down
Before the journey was done.

All the long summer day
The ghosts of noon draw nigh,
And the tremulous aspens hear
The footing of winds go by.

By the Aurelian Wall

Down to the gates of the sea,
Out of the gates of the west,
Journeys the whispering river
Before the place of his rest.

The road he loved to follow
When June came by his door,
Out through the dim blue haze
Leads, but allures no more.

The trailing shadows of clouds
Steal from the slopes and are gone;
The myriad life in the grass
Stirs, but he slumbers on;

In the Heart of the Hills

The inland wandering tern
Skreel as they forage and fly;
His loons on the lonely reach
Utter their querulous cry;

Over the floating lilies
A dragon-fly tacks and steers;
Far in the depth of the blue
A martin settles and veers;

To every roadside thistle
A gold-brown butterfly clings;
But he no more companions
All the dear vagrant things.

By the Aurelian Wall

The strong red journeying sun,
The pale and wandering rain,
Will roam on the hills forever
And find him never again.

Then twilight falls with the touch
Of a hand that soothes and stills,
And a swamp-robin sings into light
The lone white star of the hills.

Alone in the dusk he sings,
And a burden of sorrow and wrong
Is lifted up from the earth
And carried away in his song.

In the Heart of the Hills

Alone in the dusk he sings,
And the joy of another day
Is folded in peace and borne
On the drift of years away.

But there in the heart of the hills
My beautiful weary one
Sleeps where he laid him down;
And the large sweet night is begun.

AN AFTERWORD

To G. B. R.

BROTHER, the world above you
Is very fair to-day,
And all things seem to love you
The old accustomed way.

Here in the heavenly weather
In June's white arms you sleep,
Where once on the hills together
Your haunts you used to keep.

An Afterword

The idling sun that lazes
Along the open field
And gossips to the daisies
Of secrets unrevealed;

The wind that stirs the grasses
A moment, and then stills
Their trouble as he passes
Up to the darkling hills,—

And to the breezy clover
Has many things to say
Of that unwearied rover
Who once went by this way;

By the Aurelian Wall

The miles of elm-treed meadows;
The clouds that voyage on,
Streeling their noiseless shadows
From countries of the sun;

The tranquil river reaches
And the pale stars of dawn;
The thrushes in their beeches
For reverie withdrawn;

With all your forest fellows
In whom the blind heart calls,
For whom the green leaf yellows,
On whom the red leaf falls;

An Afterword

The dumb and tiny creatures
Of flower and blade and sod,
That dimly wear the features
And attributes of God;

The airy migrant comers
On gauzy wings of fire,
Those wanderers and roamers
Of indefinite desire;

The rainbirds and all dwellers
In solitude and peace,
Those lingerers and foretellers
Of infinite release;

By the Aurelian Wall

Yea, all the dear things living
That rove or bask or swim,
Remembering and misgiving,
Have felt the day grow dim.

Even the glad things growing,
Blossom and fruit and stem,
Are poorer for your going
Because you were of them.

Yet since you loved to cherish
Their pleading beauty here,
Your heart shall not quite perish
In all the golden year;

An Afterword

But God's great dream above them
Must be a tinge less pale,
Because you lived to love them
And make their joy prevail.

SEVEN WIND SONGS

*Now these are the seven wind songs
For Andrew Straton's death,
Blown through the reeds of the river,
A sigh of the world's last breath,*

*Where the flickering red auroras
Out on the dark sweet hills
Follow all night through the forest
The cry of the whip-poor-wills.*

Seven Wind Songs

For the meanings of life are many,
But the purpose of love is one,
Journeying, tarrying, lonely
As the sea wind or the sun.

I

Wind of the Northern land,
Wind of the sea,
No more his dearest hand
Comes back to me.

Wind of the Northern gloom,
Wind of the sea,
Wandering waifs of doom
Feckless are we.

By the Aurelian Wall

Wind of the Northern land,
Wind of the sea,
I cannot understand
How these things be.

II

Wind of the low red morn
At the world's end,
Over the standing corn
Whisper and bend.

Then through the low red morn
At the world's end,
Far out from sorrow's bourne,
Down glory's trend,

Seven Wind Songs

Tell the last years forlorn
At the world's end,
Of my one peerless born
Comrade and friend.

III

Wind of the April stars,
Wind of the dawn,
Whether God nears or fars,
He lived and shone.

Wind of the April night,
Wind of the dawn,
No more my heart's delight
Bugles me on.

By the Aurelian Wall

Wind of the April rain,
Wind of the dawn,
Lull the old world from pain
Till pain be gone.

IV

Wind of the summer noon,
Wind of the hills,
Gently the hand of June
Stays thee and stills.

Far off, untouched by tears,
Raptures or ills,
Sleeps he a thousand years
Out on the hills.

Seven Wind Songs

Wind of the summer noon,
Wind of the hills,
Is the land fair and boon
Whither he wills?

V

Wind of the gulfs of night,
Wind of the sea,
Where the pale streamers light
My world for me, —

Breath of the wintry Norns,
Frost-touch or sleep, —
He whom my spirit mourns
Deep beyond deep

By the Aurelian Wall

To the last void and dim
Where ages stream —
Is there no room for him
In all this dream?

VI

Wind of the outer waste,
Threne of the outer world,
Leash of the stars unlaced,
Morning unfurled,

Somewhere at God's great need,
I know not how,
With the old strength and speed
He is come now;

Seven Wind Songs

Therefore my soul is glad
With the old pride,
Tho' this small life is sad
Here in my side.

VII

Wind of the driven snow,
Wind of the sea,
On a long trail and slow
Farers are we.

Wind of the Northern gloom,
Wind of the sea,
Shall I one day resume
His love for me?

By the Aurelian Wall

Wind of the driven snow,
Wind of the sea,
Then shall thy vagrant know
How these things be.

*These are the seven wind songs
For Andrew Straton's rest,
From the hills of the Scarlet Hunter
And the trail of the endless quest.*

*The wells of the sunrise harken,
They wait for a year and a day:
Only the calm sure thrushes
Fluting the world away!*

Seven Wind Songs

*For the husk of life is sorrow;
But the kernels of joy remain,
Teeming and blind and eternal
As the hill wind or the rain.*

ANDREW STRATON

Andrew Straton was my friend,
With his Saxon eyes and hair,
And his loyal viking spirit,
Like an islesman of the North
With his earldom on the sea.

At his birth the mighty Mother
Made of him a fondling one,
Hushed from pain within her arms,
With her seal upon his lips;

Andrew Straton

And from that day he was numbered
With the sons of consolation,
Peace and cheer were in his hands,
And her secret in his will.

Now the night has Andrew Straton
Housed from wind and storm forever
In a chamber of the gloom
Where no window fronts the morning,
Lulled to rest at last from roving
To the music of the rain.

And his sleep is in the far-off
Alien villages of the dusk,
Where there is no voice of welcome
To the country of the strangers,
Save the murmur of the pines.

By the Aurelian Wall

And the fitful winds all day
Through the grass with restless footfalls
Haunt about his narrow door,
Muttering their vast unknown
Border balladry of time,
To the hoarse rote of the sea.

There he reassumes repose,
He who never learned unrest
Here amid our fury of toil,
Undisturbed though all about him
To the cohorts of the night
Sound the bugles of the spring;
And his slumber is not broken
When along the granite hills
Flare the torches of the dawn.

Andrew Straton

More to me than kith or kin
Was the silence of his speech;
And the quiet of his eyes,
Gathered from the lonely sweep
Of the hyacinthine hills,
Better to the failing spirit
Than a river land in June:
And to look for him at evening
Was more joy than many friends.

As the woodland brooks at noon
Were his brown and gentle hands,
And his face as the hill country
Touched with the red autumn sun

By the Aurelian Wall

Frank and patient and untroubled
Save by the old trace of doom
In the story of the world.
So the years went brightening by.

Now a lyric wind and weather
Breaks the leaguer of the frost,
And the shining rough month March
Crumbles into sun and rain;
But the glad and murmurous year
Wheels above his rest and wakens
Not a dream for Andrew Straton.

Now the uplands hold an echo
From the meadow lands at morn;
And the marshes hear the rivers
Rouse their giant heart once more, —

Andrew Straton

Hear the crunching floe start seaward
From a thousand valley floors;
While far on amid the hills
Under stars in the clear night,
The replying, the replying,
Of the ice-cold rivulets
Plashing down the solemn gorges
In their arrowy blue speed,
Fills and frets the crisp blue twilight
With innumerable sound, —
With the whisper of the spring.

But the melting fields are empty,
Something ails the bursting year.

By the Aurelian Wall

Ah, now helpless, O my rivers,
Are your lifted voices now!
Where is all the sweet compassion
Once your murmur held for me?
Cradled in your dells, I listened
To your crooning, learned your language,
Born your brother and your kin.

When I had the morn for revel,
You made music at my door;
Now the days go darkling on,
And I cannot guess your words.
Shall young joy have troops of neighbors,
While this grief must house alone?

Andrew Straton

O my brothers of the hills,
Who abide through stress and change,
On the borders of our sorrow,
With no part in human tears,
Lift me up your voice again
And put by this grievous thing!

Ah, my rivers, Andrew Straton
Leaves me here a vacant world!

I must hear the roar of cities
And the jargon of the schools,
With no word of that one spirit
Who was steadfast as the sun

By the Aurelian Wall

And kept silence with the stars.
I must sit and hear the babble
Of the worldling and the fool,
Prating know-alls and reformers
Busy to improve on man,
With their chatter about God;
Nowhere, nowhere the blue eyes,
With their swift and grave regard,
Falling on me with God's look.

I have seen and known and loved
One who was too sure for sorrow,
Too serenely wise for haste,
Too compassionate for scorn,
Fearless man and faultless comrade,
One great heart whose beat was love.

Andrew Straton

In a thousand thousand hollows
Of the hills to-day there twinkle
Icy-blue handbreadths of April,
Where the sinking snows decay
In the everlasting sun;
And a thousand tiny creatures
Stretch their heart to fill the world.

Now along the wondrous trail
Andrew Straton loved to follow
Day by day and year on year,
The awaited sure return
Of all sleeping forest things
Is reheralded abroad,
Till the places of their journey, —

By the Aurelian Wall

Wells the frost no longer hushes,
Ways no drift can bury now,
Wood and stream and road and hillside, —
Hail their coming as of old.

But my beautiful lost comrade
Of the golden heart, whose life
Rang through April like a voice
Through some Norland saga, crying
Skoal to death, comes not again;
Time shall not revive that presence
More desired than all the flowers,
Longer wished for than the birds.

April comes, but April's lover
Is departed and not here.

Andrew Straton

Sojourning beyond the frost,
He delays; and now no more, —
Though the goldenwings are come
With their resonant tattoo,
And along the barrier pines
Morning reddens on the hills
Where the thrushes wake before it, —
No more to the summoning flutes
Of the forest Andrew Straton
Gets him forth afoot, light-hearted,
On the unfrequented ways
With companionable Spring.

Only the old dreams return.

By the Aurelian Wall

So I shape me here this fancy,
Foolish me! of Andrew Straton;
How the lands of that new kindred
Have detained him with allegiance,
And some far day I shall find him,
There as here my only captain,
Master of the utmost isles
In the ampler straits of sea.

Out of the blue melting distance
Of the dreamy southward range
Journey back the vagrant winds,
Sure and indolent as time;
And the trembling wakened wood-flowers
Lift their gentle tiny faces

Andrew Straton

To the sunlight; and the rainbirds
From the lonely cedar barrens
Utter their far pleading cry.

Up across the swales and burnt lands
Where the soft gray tinges purple,
Mouldering into scarlet mist,
Comes the sound as of a marching,
The low murmur of the April
In the many-rivered hills.

Then there stirs the old vague rapture,
Like a wanderer come back,
Still desiring, scathed but deathless,
From beyond the bourne of tears,
Wayworn to his vacant cabin,
To this foolish fearless heart.

By the Aurelian Wall

Soon the large mild stars of springtime
Will resume the ancient twilight
And restore the heart of earth
To unvexed eternal poise;
For the great Will, calm and lonely,
Can no mortal grief derange,
No lost memories perturb;
And the sluices of the morning
Will be opened, and the daybreak
Well with bird-calls and with brook-notes,
Till there be no more despair
In the gold dream of the world.

THE GRAVE-TREE

Let me have a scarlet maple
For the grave-tree at my head,
With the quiet sun behind it,
In the years when I am dead.

Let me have it for a signal,
Where the long winds stream and stream,
Clear across the dim blue distance,
Like a horn blown in a dream;

By the Aurelian Wall

Scarlet when the April vanguard
Bugles up the laggard Spring,
Scarlet when the bannered Autumn,
Marches by unwavering.

It will comfort me with honey
When the shining rifts and showers
Sweep across the purple valley
And bring back the forest flowers.

It will be my leafy cabin,
Large enough when June returns
And I hear the golden thrushes
Flute and hesitate by turns.

The Grave-Tree

And in fall, some yellow morning,
When the stealthy frost has come,
Leaf by leaf it will befriend me
As with comrades going home.

Let me have the Silent Valley
And the hill that fronts the east,
So that I can watch the morning
Redden and the stars released.

Leave me in the Great Lone Country,
For I shall not be afraid
With the shy moose and the beaver
There within my scarlet shade.

By the Aurelian Wall

I would sleep, but not too soundly,
Where the sunning partridge drums,
Till the crickets hush before him
When the Scarlet Hunter comes.

That will be in warm September,
In the stillness of the year,
When the river-blue is deepest
And the other world is near.

When the apples burn their reddest
And the corn is in the sheaves,
I shall stir and waken lightly
At a footfall in the leaves.

The Grave-Tree

It will be the Scarlet Hunter
Come to tell me time is done;
On the idle hills forever
There will stand the idle sun.

There the wind will stay to whisper
Many wonders to the reeds;
But I shall not fear to follow
Where my Scarlet Hunter leads.'

I shall know him in the darkling
Murmur of the river bars,
While his feet are on the mountains
Treading out the smoldering stars.

By the Aurelian Wall

I shall know him, in the sunshine
Sleeping in my scarlet tree,
Long before he halts beside it
Stooping down to summon me.

Then fear not, my friends, to leave me
In the boding autumn vast;
There are many things to think of
When the roving days are past.

Leave me by the scarlet maple,
When the journeying shadows fail,
Waiting till the Scarlet Hunter
Pass upon the endless trail.

www.ingramcontent.com/pod-product-compliance
Lightning Source LLC
Chambersburg PA
CBHW021938160426
43195CB00011B/1142